Donor Conception Network

Mixed blessings: Building a family with and without donor help

By
Olivia Montuschi

Olivia Montuschi

Olivia Montuschi is the mother of two donor conceived adults, born in 1983 and 1986. She and her husband Walter Merricks founded the Donor Conception Network with four other families in 1993. Olivia trained as a teacher and counsellor and for many years worked as a parenting educator and trainer, writing materials and running parenting education programmes. She is the author of all the Telling and Talking booklets for parents of donor conceived children of different ages and has written many articles about parenting children conceived by egg, sperm and embryo donation. Olivia currently works part-time as Practice Consultant for DC Network.

Donor Conception Network

The Donor Conception Network was started in 1993 by five families who were looking for support from others in being open with their children about donor conception. Members now include married and unmarried couples, single women, same sax couples, parents who have been separated, divorced or widowed, individual adults who are donor offspring and some sperm and egg donors. About half of our members already have children and most of the others are contemplating or currently having fertility treatment with donated eggs, sperm or embryos.

We hold national meetings twice a year – with good childcare and an older children's group – have local groups in many parts of the UK, provide a contact list of parents you can 'phone or email, have a twice yearly Journal and a lively website with an interactive forum.

Do join us.

Find out more from our website www.dcnetwork.org or 'phone 020 7278 2608

Please note that in the interests of member confidentiality, the photographs used on the cover of this and the Telling and Talking brochures are sourced from photo libraries for illustrational purposes only and do not necessarily portray families created through donor conception.

Contents

Acknowledgements and thanks

This booklet could not have been written without the many families who gave up time to talk with me in person or over the 'phone. Thank you so much for being so generous in sharing your thoughts and feelings for the benefit of others.

Enormous thanks are also due to Marilyn Crawshaw, Fellow of the University of York; Jane Ellis, adoption social worker and mother to donor conceived adults; Marion Scott, DCN Steering Group member, mother to a donor conceived teenager and mentor to me for this project and Nina Barnsley, manager of DCN. All four took time and considerable trouble to read early drafts and between them nearly managed to eliminate all my long sentences. They also immeasurably improved the content and the way it is expressed.

Final thanks must go to my ever patient husband Walter.

Olivia Montuschi
January 2012

Introduction

This booklet is intended to support couples or individuals who are at any stage of creating a family that includes children conceived without the help of a donor AND with donor assistance. The two most important aims are to –

• Support you in finding ways of sharing information that feel comfortable for you and your children, no matter how they were conceived or their stage of development.

• Help you think about some of the fears that you may have when contemplating using a donor to help create an addition to your family

Families with one child conceived without help (or IVF with parents' own eggs and sperm) and one or more subsequent children with donor help, are now an established part of DC Network. Sometimes parents will also have children who are adopted or from a previous relationship and maybe these or a child by donor conception came first, with a child conceived without help being brought into a re-formed family by the new couple.

Single women and same sex couples also often have mixed families, with children having been conceived both with and without donor help in previous relationships.

Because it is the most common scenario, the main focus of this booklet is on having a second child by donor conception, usually by egg donation, when the first was conceived without donor help, but all parents with mixed families will hopefully find the contents supportive and helpful for their particular situation.

We know that couples and individuals sometimes worry about having children with different beginnings so there are sections on managing 'difference' and life with young and older children in mixed families.

As this topic has not been written about before I wanted to understand as much as possible about the experiences of real families. I talked in depth with members of seventeen families, mostly mothers but including three fathers and two teenagers as well. Eleven families were headed by a heterosexual couple, two by lesbian couples and four by solo mums. I am enormously grateful to them all for sharing their thoughts and feelings. Some families' experiences have been quoted extensively but relevant details from all the families are incorporated into the text. Some names have been changed.

All families have approved their stories as they appear. Several said they wished there had been something like this when they were contemplating donor conception. Two or three had anxieties that the existence of a booklet like this might indicate that such a way of building a family was particularly fraught with problems. They wanted me to make it very clear that it had not been like that for them. They had no regrets at all in choosing to use a donor to help complete their family.

This booklet is intended to be used in conjunction with the *Telling and Talking* booklets for parents of children of different ages.

The need to have more than one child

Most parents, given the choice, would like to have more than one child. Many feel that a first child may be lonely without a brother or sister but there is no guarantee that, like in any family, siblings will get on with each other. Women or men may also find that their need to nurture is not satisfied by one child and they hope for at least one other to make their family complete.

> Amanda and Jack had not wanted their son to be an only child but discovered that Amanda needed egg donation in order to be able to conceive a sibling. Their daughter Tamsin was born four years later. Now aged 13 and 9 the two children do not get on and live fairly parallel lives. Amanda admits ruefully that her son would probably have been very happy to be an only child.

A first child takes you from the land of lazy lie-ins at the weekend to a world of early starts, playgrounds and nursery schools and the pressure to have another child from those who have become your co-habitants of this world, can be great. Some areas of towns and cities become known as 'nappy valley' because of the high concentration of families with small children living there. Once part of this world, not producing a second child can be perceived by others as being 'selfish' and outside the norm. Then there are the expectations from within your own family. Grandparents may be hoping for another grandchild and drop heavy hints about having a second baby.

Pain of secondary infertility

Having difficulty in conceiving a second child is a pain that can be difficult for many to understand, particularly those who are struggling to conceive their first. But apart from having overcome the anxiety that you may never become a mother or father, the sadness and disappointment are no less the second time around. For some women it feels worse because of being surrounded by parents, babies and pregnant friends. There is also often worry about the reality of becoming older with all the possible risks and the fear of not having enough energy, or of standing out as an older mother.

A different family to the one envisaged

For both individuals and couples, the need to use a donor means moving on from the family that you had in mind as you entered parenthood. Before you are ready to welcome a child with a non-genetic connection into your family, you may want to give yourself time to grieve the additional child you could not have.

Finding that you are going to need to use a donor in order to conceive can add to the pain, loss and potential stigma of not being able to easily conceive a second child at all. The shock is sometimes less for those who needed IVF the first time round than for those who conceived easily. But for other people the diminished sense of self makes loss of fertility hard to bear and difficult to overcome with optimism. Egg, sperm or embryo donation brings back hope. However, it can also bring anxieties and fears of the unknown and an exaggerated variant of the worry of many second time mums and dads – can I love this child as much as my first? Do I have enough love to go round?

Louise and David

Louise and her husband David had conceived their first child with the help of IVF, but it worked first time and they assumed that this would happen when they tried again. But only a year later, and still under 40, Louise's ovarian reserve had dropped dramatically and two further IVF attempts both resulted in early miscarriages. Because of this and the fact that she had had only one follicle on each IVF cycle, her consultant recommended that she should consider donor eggs.

As they lived in an area of London that was full of families and young children, this was a very painful period of Louise's life. Friends who had been having a first baby at the same time as her were moving on to second children whilst Louise was going through the rollercoaster of fertility treatment and the heartbreak of miscarriages.

It took about eight weeks for Louise and David to decide that they would like to pursue egg donation. During this time Louise felt sad that any further child she had would not be genetically connected to her. However, she was also very hopeful that egg donation would bring them the completed family they so longed for. Louise was worried that an egg donation conceived child would not be able to connect with her in some way and would possibly reject her in the future. David's anxieties were that Louise might not feel a connection with the baby. Louise felt lucky that her clinic had a very good counsellor she could talk to whenever this felt necessary and the counsellor recommended DC Network to them. Talking with both counsellor and DCN helped Louise feel less alone as she realised that many women were having second children by egg donation.

Louise and David were fortunate enough to be able to afford to go on an accelerated egg donation waiting list at a London clinic and their donor was an egg-sharer. The daughter who resulted for Louise and David is much loved by everyone, including grandparents, uncles and aunts and god-parents who have been specially chosen as people that their daughter might feel comfortable talking to in later years. The pregnancy coincidentally took place at the same time of year as Louise's first pregnancy which helped to make it 'feel right' and she feels very fortunate to have experienced the same strong maternal bond to her daughter as to her first born child.

Fears and worries

The most common fear that we hear at DCN from women who are contemplating egg donation after having had a child without donor help, is whether they are likely to 'feel the same' about a child not genetically connected to them. The worry is that bonding will not happen in the same way and that they will not 'recognise' the child as their own.

An interesting question to contemplate is the assumption that if a child is genetically connected then this 'recognition' is automatic, leading to a deep love flowing from mother to child as surely as night follows day. This we know does not always happen: many parents of genetically connected children find that it takes several days or even weeks to 'recognise' and fall in love with their baby.

Love is not genetically programmed. We love our partners but are not genetically connected to them. My husband knew he would be able to love our sperm donor conceived children because he had come to love very much my son from my previous marriage. Of course, not all step-parents feel the same way about their partner's children.

Many of the women I talked to have said that carrying the baby or babies inside them felt so normal and right. It was a similar experience to pregnancy with their first child – bonding came easily, both during pregnancy and after birth. They were pleased that they had been able to contribute to the well-being of their donor conceived child by looking after themselves during pregnancy. The emerging science of epigenetics is also drawing attention to how some of the child's genes may be turned on or off by the environment of the womb. This may mean that whilst the fundamental blueprint of the genetic make up of a child will come from the mixture of genes from the donor and the fertile partner, some of the functions of those genes may be affected by the environment in which they develop in the mother. This is very much a case of 'watch this scientific space'.

Some women do remain anxious during their pregnancy about what a donor conceived child will look like, how well they will bond with the baby and if that child will reject them in the future. This can sometimes be associated with reluctance to tell close family and friends about the conception. It may mean that there is an element of shame or stigma about using donor conception. It is also sometimes associated with having put pressure on a partner to go ahead with having a child in a way s/he feels ambivalent about. Ideally, these issues should be addressed together, and if necessary in counselling, before donor conception takes place, but it is never too late to explore difficult feelings. This can be done by being in touch with others via DC Network, through web based support forums or seeking a counsellor through the British Infertility Counselling Association bica.net or local contacts.

Whether mothers and fathers will 'feel the same' about their donor conceived child, and any other children, is quite a different thing. All children are different and some genetically connected siblings are significantly different in looks, temperament, talents and abilities to their brothers and sisters. All manner of factors can influence how parents feel about each of their children – gender, birth order, how the temperament of the child fits with that of the parent, what is going on for parents as individuals or as a couple and what is happening in the wider world as well, such as parents' employment or housing situation.

Experience from the field of adoption with families that include adopted and birth children, shows that a majority of parents feel that the relationship with each child is similar. A small number describe the relationship with each child as 'different' but that the difference was in nature not depth. A typical comment from parents was, *"They are all my children. I love them but they are all different"*.

Difference

The words 'difference or different' have come up time and again in the descriptions and explorations above. Difference is often perceived as something to be avoided if at all possible; parents worry that their child may feel uncomfortable or be given a hard time by others because of the way they came into the family. What will be true, however, is that your children will have different beginnings to each other. The meaning that is placed on this by you, your wider family and ultimately all your children, is key to the impact this has on your family life.

Difference does not have to be negative. Difference can be exciting, stimulating, a cause of celebration or it can be relatively neutral… something that just is… and accepted as that. Difference is only worrying or dangerous if we feel threatened by it or someone is threatening us because of it.

One family where difference is writ large is that of Jackie and her partner Richard. Jackie has a daughter Isabel, now 12, conceived without help in a previous relationship. When she was a solo mum she had twins Daniel and James by double (egg and sperm) donation. They are now six. Richard has an 18 year-old mixed race daughter Jasmine from a previous relationship. When the children of the family are all together, they look very different to one another. The boys are fraternal twins and so do not look much alike but despite having different temperaments and talents, they get on very well together, as do all the children.

With the age gaps of six years, making time for each child can be difficult and life is emotionally demanding. However, Jackie feels that there is a balance in the family. Each adult has a daughter from a previous relationship and both girls see their other parent regularly. The boys are not genetically linked to either Jackie or Richard but they are to each other. The girls come and go from the house but the boys are always around. Jackie feels that this situation might be difficult for a single child but together the boys manage it well.

Whilst flexibility, unflappability and good organisation are keys to managing this big family, it is Jackie and Richard's laid-back attitude to 'difference' that makes it a cohesive and happy whole.

One of the mothers I talked to has a well-controlled mental illness, as well as being the mother of egg donation twins and an older child conceived without any help. I didn't know about her condition when I spoke with her but she dropped it into conversation when an appropriate moment came up and later told me that she does the same with her twin's origins. No stigma about either for her.

How we manage difference will depend on many things. Our own background and experiences will be important influences. If our parents were fearful of change or difference in others and perhaps inflexible in their attitudes, then we may pick up their approach to life. This is not inevitable for people brought up in cautious families, who can find themselves challenging the narrow boundaries in which they were raised. Doing something 'different' like having a child with a non-genetic connection could feel exciting, even liberating, or it might bring back to the surface fearful feelings from an earlier time. If it is the latter, then this could be an indication that adding to your family by donor conception is not for you. On the other hand it could also be that some good, supportive counselling could help with thinking through what 'difference' means to you and whether it is possible to manage this without detriment to the family.

How does the capacity to become comfortable with difference come about? The mother I referred to above feels at ease with having children from different origins because secondary infertility and the contemplation of egg donation was the second crisis that she and her husband faced together. The first was the diagnosis of her mental illness. Having weathered this together and developed very good communication 'antennae' between them, she feels they can manage anything now. They are both thrilled with their young family.   Like other mums and dads who feel comfortable with their mixed origins families, these parents have a flexibility of approach. And that is likely to mean that they will be able to adapt to the needs of their children, whatever those needs happen to be.

Going through difficult times together can mean that couples emerge with a stronger, more mature relationship. Facing what, at the time, can feel like impossible decisions together, can result in a better understanding of strengths and weaknesses between partners and improved communication. These qualities are invaluable when it comes to managing difference. Another under-recognised and under-rated capacity is that of being able to ask for help when you are in difficulties without feeling less of a person. Couples and individuals who have a good enough sense of self to know when they need help and how to find it, are more likely to be able to acknowledge difference without feeling threatened.

Fertility issues and all the difficult decision making around donor conception, can test relationships to breaking point. Not all survive. Many that do will be stronger. But even in these families it is sometimes the case that pre-conception worries re-emerge after a baby has been born. It is increasingly recognised that parenting following significant infertility can be very different to parenting where children were conceived easily. Kate Brian's 2011 book *Precious Babies: Pregnancy, Birth and Parenting after Infertility* acknowledges this. Support is always available from DC Network where we can put you in touch with others or recommend a counsellor to help you make sense of troubling or puzzling feelings.

There are passages in the *Telling and Talking 0-7* and *8-11* booklets to help with talking about 'difference' with your children if this is a question that arises in your family.

When to start 'telling' family and others about the need for a donor

Most people like to know that their family are behind them when making major decisions, like having donor conception, but often feel anxious when sharing information. Sometimes people worry about disappointing their own parents or being disapproved of for choosing an unconventional way to make or complete their family. Where there is already a genetically connected child, will grandparents and other family members treat a donor conceived child in the same way?

Our experience at DC Network and from research included in *Relative Strangers*, a lovely and very readable book based on research that includes grandparents feelings about having a donor conceived child in the family, is that on the whole grandparents are enormously supportive of their adult children. They want what is best for them. If they know about difficulties in conceiving a second child they may be more open to ways of making this possible than their adult children imagine. They could be reassured by knowing that their offspring are thinking through all the short and long-term implications for the whole family of having a child in this way. All the families I talked to said that close family members had been anxious but supportive beforehand. Then the new (donor conceived) members of the family had been welcomed like any other child. Most recipient couples told their parents and siblings about their need for donor conception either before they had treatment or in early pregnancy, so that there was plenty of time for relatives to get used to the idea before a child was born.

The small number of families I talked to had the backing of their parents. We do know of others where some family members will probably never understand or accept the need for donor conception. There are lots of reasons for this but clues to potential problems can lie in having had past clashes over respect of difference. It can be painful, but in some circumstances the new family has to make decisions that are right for them: this may mean leaving behind those who find it difficult to be supportive. The *Telling and Talking Family and Friends* book can be helpful in thinking through how you might want to talk with relatives and friends about what you are doing and the *Our Family* book is designed to help your parents, siblings and friends understand more about donor conception and what it might mean for the whole family. Both books have tips at the end about what is and is not helpful to say.

The chapter on *Talking with Others in Telling and Talking 0 – 7* gives general guidance on telling and is as appropriate to mixed families as it is for those without a genetically connected first child.

Telling and the question of looks

It is a very good idea to share information before birth with those who matter to you in order to minimise comparisons between the siblings and with regard to who the new baby looks like. People just seem to be programmed to make these comments. It can, therefore, be helpful if those you are close to understand about the non-genetic factor. Sometimes donor conceived children look very different to the first child and sometimes they don't. Louise said that the one thing that can get her down on a bad day is comments about how different her (egg-donor conceived) daughter looks from her and her older child. Mostly she says to those who mention it, that her husband was also very blonde as a baby and she laughs off comments from strangers and acquaintances. She did mention that differences in looks were the one thing she had not thought about in advance.

Another parent I spoke to said that her boy/girl twins were very different in looks and nature. They were conceived in Spain and the girl looks typically Spanish whilst the boy looks just like his dad and older brother. They too get unsought after comments from people in supermarket queues, for example, but have found these situations relatively easy to respond to lightly.

Amanda's children look very different. Her son Matthew was conceived without donor help and her daughter Tamsin conceived by egg donation in Spain. Amanda was told that she had been matched with a donor whose colouring was like hers, but in fact Tamsin is very Mediterranean looking unlike Matthew who looks a lot like his mum. Amanda does not draw attention to this resemblance with her son because she worries about Tamsin feeling 'different', but she does wonder if this is the right approach.

Some parents have decided that commenting in a very matter of fact way about resemblances in looks, talents and traits in the family is more helpful than avoiding the whole conversation, something which may be noticeable by its absence (it being very common in families to talk about likenesses). There is always a balance to be struck between this and the potential for hurt when mentioned.

Of course people in families where all the children are genetically related can look very different to each other, but there is a heightened sensitivity to questions about looks when donor conception is involved.

Telling the older child

Another frequent worry we hear from parents is about when, how and what to tell their older child or children about the way the younger one was conceived. The main concern tends to be about compromising the privacy of the younger child. It is feared that this might happen by telling the older one about the help that they had to have the new baby, before the younger child is capable of understanding their origins for him or herself.

If there is a big gap in ages between the two children, there is a danger that the older child will be reaching adolescence if 'telling' is delayed until the younger child is old enough to understand. Teenage years are not a good age to be starting to share information of this sort and the older child might also resent not having been told earlier. Parents worry that giving information about donor conception provides ammunition for the older child to feel superior to their younger sibling (because of the full genetic connection) and possibly use it to tease their little brother or sister.

DC Network has no evidence so far that donor conceived children mind that others know about their origins before they do. This is because children who are 'told' early accept their story as 'just who they are' and have fewer reasons to be concerned about who else knows. They, and their older siblings do not have the same worries as their parents as they do not share their fertility history. In fact, it can be helpful for younger children if others around them have an early understanding about their conception: they can treat this information in a matter of fact way and talk with the child about it, should the subject come up. Parents know their own children best. They need to use their own judgement, sharing the information in a simple, matter-of-fact and age appropriate way with older children. This can either fully inform them or prepare the ground for more information later when the younger one is ready to hear the story too.

If the age gap between children is around three years then reading one of the *Our Story* books together may be a good way to normalise the conception of the younger child with both children. Prior to this, parents can prepare the ground with the older child by using some of the appropriate age starter language from the *Telling and Talking* books. If the older child was conceived by IVF, then there is an additional piece of information to bring into the younger child's story –

"We always wanted to have more than one child but by the time we were ready to have another baby mummy's eggs weren't working properly any more and we needed a very kind woman to give us some of her eggs to help make....... The doctor then mixed these eggs with daddy's sperm, in the same way as they did to make you, and the embryo that the eggs and sperm made was put into my tummy and grew into......"

Despite explaining about the donation, where children are relatively close in age it will be many years before the penny drops that one of them is not genetically connected to both parents or perhaps neither of them. Where the topic has been on the family conversation agenda all the while then the realisation should be a slow dawning rather than a sudden shock and, therefore, accepted more readily by each child.

Teasing amongst siblings is normal behaviour. The oldest can sometimes try to assert their rank or authority in ways that are not very kind to younger brothers or sisters. Unless they have reason to feel very resentful of their sibling for other reasons, they are unlikely to use origins information to deliberately hurt them. However, their understanding about the full implications of the non-genetic connection of their younger sibling will develop earlier. Parents could try to keep track of what the elder child might be saying to the younger, but this is not always easy. When I was talking with parents who had older children as part of their mixed family I came across instances of children not getting on together, looking different and just being very different people, but no-one reported any sign of teasing or bullying based on genetic difference. Defuse potentially difficult situations between your children with a sense of humour and try to treat remarks lightly but authoritatively, particularly as they get older.

Telling the younger child

It is important to acknowledge the difference between each of your children's conceptions with younger children from an early age. This is because older children are likely to have been told about the help that their parents needed to have their younger sibling. This can be done with simple language like, *"We needed this special help to have you, but we didn't need it to have........ Sometimes this happens."* added to the usual wording used to explain donor conception to young children, given in *Telling and Talking 0 - 7* and the *Our Story books*. If IVF was used to conceive both children you can tell the story about this. Then simply add that the egg that helped to make the younger child came from a very kind woman because mummy's eggs weren't working properly by the time she was ready to have another baby.

Some donor conceived children are sad for a while when they come to realise that they do not have a genetic link to both parents: that they are not connected 'by blood' to a much loved mum or dad. This might also include sadness (or delight, depending on the relationship at the time) that their older sibling is only half related 'by blood' too. Listening and acknowledgement of feelings, whatever they are, will go a long way to helping with this.

Life with young children

One of the striking differences between the families I talked to was between families who had donor conceived twins and those who had just one child with the help of a donor. All the families were caught up in the frenzy and fun of life with young children. Those with twins definitely found that 'twin issues' were much more dominant in their lives than anything to do with donor conception. But, those with twins also said that they were very pleased to have two children by donation so that they would have each other to talk to about their conception later in life. It was clear that it was comforting to parents to know this. These feelings overcame some of the less positive feelings about having two children at once. Of course each twin may feel very differently about their conception as they grow older and this could have an impact on finding information about their donor or registering to be in touch with half siblings.

As in all families with more than one child, parents can feel differently about each twin. In the family with twins conceived in Spain the mother was very aware of having a different relationship with her daughter who looks typically Spanish and has a different temperament to the two boys. However, she feels this is more to do with her being a girl and not to do with the origin of her looks. The boy twin looks very much like his dad and his older brother but there are many ways in which the brothers are different too. Both parents are excited by all three children's different characteristics and very open to them developing interests and hobbies that appeal to them as individuals.

I asked parents with twins by donation about equality of treatment. They either said they were far too busy to think about such things or that they were much more concerned about finding time to give attention to their eldest, rather than trying to make life equal for their donor conceived children.

Louise, whose story was told earlier, was very glad that her egg donor conceived baby is a girl and her eldest child a boy. She felt that the gender difference might help diffuse potential sibling rivalry that could become tinged with one-upmanship about genetic connection if both had been boys. Louise was also concerned to make sure that her second child was treated absolutely equally to the first one, even down to attempting to take the same number of baby photos and buying new clothes and toys rather than relying on 'hand-me-downs'.

When it's sperm rather than egg donation: or the child by donation comes first

Stuart and Stephanie

Stuart and Stephanie conceived their first son Mark by donor sperm about ten years ago. Stuart had severe male factor problems and following five unsuccessful IVF/ICSI attempts over about four years, in desperation they finally decided to use donor help to start their family. Stuart found adjusting to the reality of his fertility difficulties and the need to use a donor very difficult but when Mark was born they bonded well and the two have a very good relationship.

When Stuart and Stephanie discussed having a second child, Stuart was very keen to try ICSI again, as techniques had refined in the intervening years. Stephanie, however, felt that they should use a donor so that their children would be on an equal footing in the family. The situation remained unresolved for some time, there was a lot of tension as each partner stuck to his and her position and the relationship between Stuart and Stephanie suffered. Finally Stephanie agreed to try ICSI again with Stuart's sperm and she conceived their second son Martin. The boys are six years apart in age but get on well.

Because of the age gap it was possible to start talking with Mark about his new sibling and the differences between how they were conceived whilst Stephanie was pregnant with Martin. Both parents treat the whole issue very matter of factly and talk about the information belonging to the family rather than one child or the other. They have always been very open about their family origins. All family and friends know but, like many other DCN members, they find that friends tend to forget.

On the question of potential favouritism, Stuart feels that he does not favour Martin in any way and very much enjoys more grown-up conversations about football and other shared interests with Mark. He says, "It is much more important that I am a good father to Mark rather than his biological father".

Stephanie continues to worry about how her children will manage the inequality in genetic relationships as they grow up and how Mark will feel when he realises at some point how much his dad wanted to be a biological father. This wish, of course, was nothing to do with rejection of Mark but because Stuart needed to know for his own sense of self that he could father a child.

Another family, who live outside of the UK, used donor sperm for a second child because of serious antibody incompatibility problems in a first (IVF) pregnancy leading to a very anaemic and underweight baby. Jenny, the mother, told me her first son was a very easy, calm baby and the second cried a lot and was more difficult. She found it easier to relate to her first child who is more like her and was very aware of the second being donor conceived and the fear of the unknown in his character. She told me she was conscious of him being different and it is only as he has got older and his own personality has developed that she feels she has got to know him. Jenny commented to me that as she is an only child she has no experience of children in a family being very different, having differing needs, quarrelling etc. and she found this difficult. The children's father has been much more relaxed about differences between his two sons and curious to see how his second son's personality would develop.

Although family and close friends know about the donor conception, Jenny talks to her sons in English about their origins. As they live in a non-English speaking country they speak another language at school. Jenny feels that this will give them protection from teasing until they are old enough to 'own' their information.

A story of embryo donation first

Sarah and Paul's journey to their family has been a very, very long one. Like many people they have had multiple unsuccessful IVF cycles and miscarriages. Unlike many others they became approved adopters, although they did not go on to adopt a child. However, like Daniela in another story, they felt that nothing prepared them for donor conception like going through the adoption preparation process. Because of this it was very important for them to stay in the UK for their treatment so that their children can have access to their donors later if they choose to do so.

In fact only one of Sarah and Paul's children will have to choose the search option from age 18. James, the eldest, was conceived by embryo donation whereas Toby was conceived by IVF but without donor help. When it came to trying for a sibling for James, Sarah at first used more of the 10 frozen embryos that had been donated in her cycle that produced James, but it wasn't to be. When her fertility doctor said that he thought he could help her become pregnant without donor help, Sarah was concerned about the difference there would be between her children, but at that point didn't think the treatment would work. When she became pregnant she and Paul were thrilled but Sarah worried that she would not love this baby as much as she loved her first (non-genetically connected) child. When Toby was born she was pleased to find that she had plenty of love to go round.

James is now 6 and Toby 2 and Sarah and Paul often have to remind themselves that there is a difference in their boy's beginnings. It probably helps that the physical 'fit' in the family is good. Sarah is always being told how much James looks like her. She knows he doesn't but family photographs show parents and children with similar colouring. With the help of Photobox Sarah has made books for each child explaining how much they were wanted and their particular story. They were both conceived by IVF at the same clinic and only one page, mentioning the embryo donation, differs James' story from that of Toby.

Both Sarah and Paul know that they are likely to face a lot of questions in the future. The boys are very different people and, as with most parents of more than one child, they will face the issue of wanting to treat them equally whilst also catering to the very different needs of each child. They attended a DC Network Telling and Talking workshop that confirmed their instinct to be very open with their children. They are also planning to use the book *Hope and Will Have a Baby* about embryo donation to help explain to James about his beginnings. This book is suitable for children from six or seven as it has slightly more text and longer explanations than the *Our Story* series, which is for younger children. There are also *Hope and Will* books that cover other donation types.

Like most families, Sarah and Paul would not have chosen the differences their family have, but now they are here, they are embracing them and even contemplating adding to their family by embryo donation again.

A view into the future

In one family I talked with, Zara the eldest child is 17 and was present when I spoke with her mum Jane. The donor conceived children are egg donation non-identical girl twins of 10. Zara spoke about the difference in looks between her and her sisters. She would prefer it if they looked alike but found it difficult to explain why she thought this. She is closer to one twin than the other because of personality and interests. However, it is the age gap that makes most difference. When she was ten herself she 'hated them' for getting in the way and into her things.

What came through strongly in the conversation with Jane and Zara was that twin rather than donor conception issues have dominated the family over the last ten years. Difficulties relating to twins as individuals and the sheer time and space they take up means that donor conception is relegated to a minor part in family life. Jane realised recently that despite having talked very openly over the years about their egg donation origins, the twins still made assumptions about likenesses that would link them with her extended family. This may or may not be evidence that they still have not grasped the essence of the non-genetic connections in their family. They may both 'know' and 'not know' this information at the same time, but it is important for them emotionally and socially to link with Jane's family through likeness. I suspect that biology lessons in secondary school will clarify matters intellectually. It may, however, not make any difference to their behaviour or references within the extended family.

In my own family there is an age gap of twelve years between my son from my first marriage and our first donor conceived child. Then there is a three year age difference between our first and second donor conceived child. These three now adult children are all technically half-siblings, being genetically related to me but not to my husband, who has been step-father to our eldest since he was four. His father has not been around since he was a year old. They are all very different people and do not necessarily get along all of the time, but they do absolutely regard each other as brothers and sister and have a terrific loyalty to each other and my husband and I. The fact of their half genetic connection never comes up and has never been used as a weapon, even when relations between them have been at their most hostile.

The long view of two open families

Lily

Lily is now 18. Her brother Ben is a couple of years older. Their dad Peter contracted mumps during his wife Ellen's pregnancy with Ben and this made him infertile. Lily was conceived by donor sperm and her parents started to tell her about her origins when she was four. By the age of seven or eight she had a good understanding that she was not connected 'by blood' to Peter and that Ben was made in a different way to her. At the age of eight she wrote a letter to a man considering being a sperm donor – featured in the agony aunt column of a national newspaper – to reassure him that he would be giving the gift of life and that this was 'like charity, only better'.

Ellen and Peter had been comfortable with their choice of donor conception to have a child to complete their family and could see no reason to hide this fact from their children or others. Their comfort has clearly percolated down to Lily and Ben because, like my own children, they have always regarded each other completely as brother and sister and have never used the fact of their different ways of coming into the family against each other. Lily has appeared in national newspapers and on radio to talk about being donor conceived. Like our daughter 'Zannah she quite enjoys being 'different' but also sometimes wonders what all the fuss is about.

Dave and Emma

Dave and Emma had their son Rory by sperm donation seventeen years ago. This was a second marriage for Dave and he has a daughter, Mary, conceived without help, from his first marriage. Mary is now 34 and has two children of her own. Dave became infertile at some point in the fifteen years between Mary's conception and trying to conceive in his marriage to Emma. Dave's ex-wife also remarried and has a son. Mary was told at age 13 about the help that her dad and step-mum had needed to have Rory. Mary and Rory have always got on well and consider each other to be brother and sister although there is no genetic link between them. Rory babysits for Mary's children these days.

Rory was brought up knowing about his origins but it was only when he was 13 that he realised there was no genetic connection between himself and his sister. This was probably the result of biology lessons at school prompting the thought process in his maturing brain. The realisation did not change anything in his relationship with Mary.

Temperamentally, Dave thinks that he is like Mary, while his wife is like Rory. When Dave came into conflict with Rory during his adolescence, he caught himself wondering whether their frequent arguments were anything to do with the fact that Rory was donor-conceived. He found it helpful to recall that he had very similar difficulties with Mary when she was about the same age.

When his daughter was pregnant with her first child, Dave found himself wondering what the child would be like and particularly if s/he would have his hair. Rory has hair like his mother. Although Dave stresses the prime importance of social and emotional ties, he is aware of the power of genetic connections and how societal assumptions as well as the reality about these links can influence our thinking. Happily, everyone featured in this story, including Dave's first wife and family, get on well. The two families visit each other from time-to-time and sometimes spend Christmas together.

Having a daughter with whom he has a genetic link and a son with whom he has no genetic link has caused Dave to be more thoughtful than he otherwise might have been about the differences between the two relationships. In particular, it has caused him to examine his relationship with Rory, his donor-conceived son. That there is a difference is self-evident, he thinks. Also, he believes that the genetic aspect of this difference can only be bridged by celebrating Rory's relationship to his donor, whether or not he ever finds out who the donor is, or indeed makes contact with him.

Solo mothers and lesbian families

Single women and lesbian couples may well have children from previous relationships that have ended before they enter upon parenthood by donor conception. Or have had a known donor for one child and an anonymous or identifiable one for the second. These first children may or may not currently have contact with their father but they will probably know who he is or will be able to find him in the future. If they are in contact and see their father regularly then their situation will be very different to that of a child conceived with help from an anonymous donor. The challenges for single women are great in that they have to manage their situation without the support of a partner. In lesbian couple families there are two parents but the relationships they have to juggle on a daily basis can be very complex.

Lesbian couples and single women sometimes feel that having a donor who is known to them may be helpful for a child. This can be a very good arrangement in many cases but it is vital that each party has a watertight understanding of the intentions of the other and that the expectations fit. It is a good idea to have sessions with a counsellor and/or solicitor specialising in fertility law that results in a written agreement that is signed by all parties. This cannot be binding in law as any court will put the interests of a child as they are at that moment before any agreement made by adults, but it is valuable in setting out intentions. There are now a number of solicitors firms that specialise in fertility law.

Gemma: A solo mother's experience

Gemma and Ben's relationship was always complicated by the fact that Ben worked and preferred to live in the Far East. Gemma conceived her daughter Layla within her marriage to Ben. When they separated amicably so that he could live out there permanently, he offered to be a sperm donor for Gemma so that she could have the second child she longed for. After several unsuccessful rounds of IVF it became clear that Gemma also needed donated eggs and at this point Ben withdrew his support.

Gemma turned to the internet for information on double and embryo donation and found a supportive community that gave her a lot of information about clinics abroad. She ended up going to the Czech Republic for embryo donation where she conceived her son James.

When I spoke to Gemma she was very honest in admitting how desperate she had been to have another baby and how after all the loss and pain of the past few years embryo donation seemed like not only the solution to her problems but also the 'easiest' thing in the world to do. She had been supported by her UK clinic in going abroad for treatment but they had not offered her counselling around the implications of doing so. She told me that counselling probably would not have stopped her but it would have helped her understand what she was taking on. Three years on, she has now completed a course of counselling to help her face all the big questions she did not know she needed to address earlier. She feels it has been vitally important for her to get herself as 'OK' as possible with the decisions she made, albeit after the event. This has taken a huge amount of mental and emotional energy but she has learned how important it is to do the work, and that retrospectively was possibly the only way it was going to happen for her.

Layla, who is now 10, knows how her brother was conceived and Gemma talks to both children using the term 'whom we will never know' with regard to James' donors. Layla sees her father only once or twice a year with occasional Skype conversations in between, so essentially both children are without a father, although Layla will always know who her father is and have a relationship of some sorts with him. Gemma has found that DCN language from the *Telling and Talking* and *Our Story* books regarding fathers has been useful for talking to James, but until she had completed her counselling she sometimes had painful fantasies of James in the Czech Republic 'looking for Daddy'.

Gemma's family and two close friends all know how James was conceived and are supportive. Others assume that she used a UK sperm donor and she doesn't confirm or deny this. Both children look quite alike so unlike some of the heterosexual couples in this booklet, attention is not drawn to their different origins because of colouring or strikingly different features.

Living in a small rural community these similarities make it easier for Gemma and the children to fit in, although she does not know how much information Layla shares with friends.

Lisa, Jasmine and Mia

Lisa had a daughter Jasmine with her former partner Tony. The break-up between the couple was amicable and Tony has continued to be very involved in their daughter's life.

Lisa really wanted another child and when a suitable partner didn't come along she decided to have a child by donor conception. She was now 43 and unfortunately found that her eggs had run out of time, so her second daughter Mia was conceived by double donation in Spain. Both her donors were anonymous.

All went well for the first couple of years. Jasmine enjoyed having a little sister but she also enjoyed sibling-free time with her dad. At first Mia liked having her mum to herself but after she started nursery at around two she started assuming that Jasmine's dad was her dad too. She saw Jasmine getting excited when he arrived at the house and she would get excited as well. She found it very difficult to understand when Tony didn't want to be called Daddy by her or take her out with Jasmine. Tony's parents also saw Jasmine and gave her presents, whilst there was nothing for Mia.

By the time Mia was 3 Lisa began to realise that the lack of parity in having actual relationships with a dad and his parents plus the potential for not being able to know genetic relatives in the future, might cause significant problems for Mia as well as possible friction between the sisters. Lisa has always talked with Mia about her having a kind man and a kind woman who helped to make her, but decided that she needed to do a bit more to try and even up the situation between the siblings. First of all she talked with Tony and he agreed that Mia could sometimes be included in outings with Jasmine, as long as Jasmine was happy about that, which she was. On the weekends when Jasmine saw her dad on her own, Lisa drafted in her brother Tom to do an activity with Mia so that she didn't feel left out and had her own 'dad figure'. When Tom was unavailable she made sure that she and Mia did something special together. Now that Mia is older she understands that Tony is not her Dad, and Tom is Uncle Tom. She enjoys the company of both of them and has stopped asking for a dad. Lisa's parents have also agreed to take a more active part in Mia's life, sometimes taking the little sister out for the day when big sister Jasmine is with her dad's parents.

Mia is now nearly 7 and she is a robust little girl with a good sense of self but Lisa knows that the future may bring episodes of anger, jealousy and sadness that Jasmine knows so much about and has contact with all her genetic family and she does not. On the other hand it is perfectly possible that Mia will continue to feel comfortable in herself, enjoying her relationship with her sister and remaining close to her uncle and her mum's parents, who don't care a bit that she is not genetically related to them. Lisa wishes she had thought a bit more about the possible consequences of using anonymous donors to have Mia, but she is a resourceful woman and is clearly doing a great job of raising the girls.

This sort of situation is a particular issue for single women but can occur in both lesbian and heterosexual couples where there is a significant disparity between the actual relationships and knowledge about genetic relatives in children growing up in the same family.

Daniela and Esme

Daniela was 50 when she conceived her daughter Esme by double donation in London. She already had a son Philip in her marriage that had ended in divorce following many attempts to conceive a second child and the consideration of adoption and egg donation.

When Daniela went ahead with double donation on her own her ex-husband tried to influence Philip against her, but luckily as her son matured he came to see his mother's point of view. Philip is now 18 and gets on very well with his little sister. They do not look alike, Philip taking after his mother with brown eyes and Esme being blonde and blue eyed.

The earlier thinking that Daniela had done about adoption helped her understand about the importance of openness and forward planning. She has talked with Esme since she was very little and Esme has asked if it will be possible for her to meet her donors. Daniela has been pleased to be able to tell her that she hopes this will be possible when she is older if she still wants this.

Daniela is proud of the decisions she has taken and hopes to be an inspiration to other older women. She told me that she thoroughly enjoyed being pregnant a second time and to have faced difficult situations that she had not even imagined when making her decisions.

Jess and Dom: Mother and son in a lesbian family

Jess had her son Dom by anonymous donor insemination when she was with her former partner Maggie. Maggie already had two sons from a relationship with a man she had never actually lived with but who was and remains an active father to the boys, now young men of 25 and 22. Dom is now 16 and his mother Jess is in a civil partnership with Susie, who has three children from her former heterosexual marriage. Two of these children are at university and the other lives with Jess, Susie and Dom. However, Dom spends three nights a week with Maggie, who remains a second mum to him. Various ex-partners have re-married or are in relationships and Maggie's two sons have half siblings.

The model of family that Dom has been brought up with is that of responsible shared care. This operates on practical, financial and emotional levels. All the adults involved are committed to the children and young people in their care and are very open with them about differences, which are acknowledged and valued.

Jess and Susie are both social workers and Maggie a senior teacher and their professional trainings have contributed towards their confidence and ability to manage their complicated personal lives.

The only child in this extended family who does not know who his father is is Dom. When he was younger he expressed frustration about the law that would not allow him to know who his donor, or 'dad' as he refers to him, is. Continual badgering of the clinic where she conceived, brought Jess further information about Dom's donor and a highly prized donor number (this being before the HFEA forbade clinics to give these numbers to parents). One of the new pieces of information was that the donor came from New Zealand. This has made a huge difference to Dom, who now associates himself with this country and wears a talisman round his neck that was brought back for him by a family friend. His sense of identity has been helped considerably by having this information.

At primary school, where the vast majority of children were Muslim, Dom had a hard time with regard to the sexuality of his parents and the fact that he did not know his father. Jess supported him by making a point of reiterating whatever Dom said to others – such as not knowing his father – but resisted elaborating, even under quite close questioning from other parents. When the class and household were making Father's Day cards, she explained to Dom that she did not have a good relationship with her father (who is not comfortable with her sexuality or donor conception) and mother and son made a point of having a day out together.

Dom found secondary school easier as the children were from much more mixed backgrounds and his older sister – one of Susie's children – acted as his champion. Dom enjoys being part of his large family, currently does not talk much about being donor conceived but before university is planning to spend at least part of a gap year in New Zealand.

Diana: A tale of known and unknown sperm donors in a lesbian family

Diana had been in a relationship with Angela for seven years when they decided they would like to start a family together. A known donor was preferred as being better for a child and Diana, who was to be the biological mother, went along with Angela's choice of donor because she wanted her to have a sense of control and inclusion. The donor was Steven, a gay man known to both women, but more part of Angela's friendship circle. It took about a year of home inseminations for Diana to conceive but on the day that Diana told Angela she was pregnant, Angela ended their relationship. Diana was expecting Steven's baby and was now alone. It was during this vulnerable period that Steven appeared to re-interpret the original arrangement that he would not have much day to day involvement with the child's upbringing and as Diana said ruefully to me, you cannot legislate for the emotional impact of having a child.

Sam, the baby Diana gave birth to is now ten and has a reasonable relationship with Steven. However, over the years Diana has struggled with Steven's inability to see things from either her or Sam's perspective. His demands that Sam call him Dad before he was ready to do so; the bringing of inappropriate presents and attempts to invoke the law in order to get his way, have all meant that Diana's life has often been dominated by having to manage a relationship with Steven that she had not expected.

A new relationship in Diana's life almost came to grief as a result of the constant presence of Steven or members of his family, but eventually this settled down and the two women decided they would like to have a child together. Diana and her partner entered negotiations with a gay couple but withdrew when they realised that despite having stated their expectations very clearly at the start, the gay couple were looking for a co-parenting arrangement.

Diana's daughter Ellie was conceived with sperm from an identifiable donor at a clinic in London. Ellie is now 4 and is an exuberant, strong-willed little girl who has a rich fantasy life that includes a father who lives behind a red door and has a dog. There is quite a lot of information available about her donor and Diana will share this with Ellie when she gets older.

Diana was clear with me that having a known donor for Sam was a decision she and Angela made with the very best of intentions, but it has turned out to be much harder than she ever anticipated. Raising Ellie without the interference of a donor father has been much more straightforward. She knows that there may well come a time when Ellie will be angry with her for making the decision to use a donor through a clinic, but her donor does appear to be someone of integrity from the information he has given and hopefully will be available to Ellie when she is 18. It is also likely that half-siblings will become known too. Diana hopes that Sam will be able to say in the future that it has been important to him to know who his father is and have contact with him and his family. This may help her feel better about all the complications that have been brought into her life by having to manage the relationship with Steven.

Through various networks, Diana and her partner know a lot of lesbian couples who have children by donor conception, most using a gay known donor. Of all these people, only one family have had a really good experience. In all other cases, innocent and well-meaning assumptions of the roles each person would play, have been confounded by the unexpected emotions involved in becoming a parent and the complexity of life with a child. There also seems to be a level of emotional immaturity in most of these donors in that they have expectations of a child filling an emotional space in their lives, but difficulty in understanding the views, needs and perspective of the child and the adults bringing the child up.

Difference is writ large for this family but despite this the children seem secure, confident and emotionally stable. Their base with their parents is solid and each is managing, in their own age appropriate ways, the different knowledge of their biological backgrounds. They live in London and are surrounded at school and elsewhere by the multi-dimensional relationships and 'coats of many colour' that make up the modern family. They fit in and are loved.

Final words

You have met a true cross section of 'mixed families' in the course of reading this booklet. I hope some of them have helped you think about your own situation. What unites them all is their acceptance of 'difference' and their willingness and enthusiasm to embrace this and make life for their children and whole family as good as it can possibly be. All the parents understand that their children may go through times of questioning, sadness, confusion or anger in the future – this includes their genetically connected children as well – and they accept this is part of the parenting role that all parents face, as well as a consequence of the decisions they have made about family creation. Two of the families found that becoming approved adopters helped them think about the future from the perspective of their children. This draws attention to the differences between making the decision to have a child with or without donor help. The latter is a purely personal decision by two people whose child will share their heredity. The former involves the future of a person who will not fully share the genetic makeup of their legal parent(s). DC Network's *Preparation for DC Parenthood* workshops are not as rigorous as preparation for adoption, but they do encourage people to look at the world through the eyes of their future child. If you have not yet embarked on treatment or have yet to conceive, you may want to consider attending a workshop first.

A DCN national conference in Leeds had the theme *Feeling Comfortable, Building Confidence*, these being the cornerstones of successful donor conception parenting. One of the speakers, Jane Ellis, an adoption social worker and mother to two sperm donor conceived young men, quoted two key points from Joseph Rowntree Trust research findings about the sort of parenting that helps to build comfortable and confident families.

"Warm, authoritative and responsive parenting is usually crucial in building resilience. Parents who develop open, participative communication, problem-centred coping, confidence and flexibility tend to manage stress well and help their family to do the same"

"Available research suggests that parents...play a pivotal role in promoting the knowledge, skills and environment that can help children cope with adversity."
David Utting for the Joseph Rowntree Foundation 2007

Jane emphasised she was not saying that it was desirable for parents to do their job well by eliminating problems and issues for our children. If this happened, then we as parents would have failed in one of our most important tasks, that of helping our children cope with adversity.

The point of developing the qualities and skills explored in this booklet is to give our children the tools to face, manage and make sense of difficulties that may arise from any area of their lives. Difficulties, which may, for some, include being part of a mixed origins family. Having these tools does not guarantee a pain-free life. But with them long-term harm is less likely to result from a period of difficulty. Life is likely to be richer for having chosen the path *through* rather than *round* a problem.

Remember that most of the challenges that come up in the lives of you and your children are likely to have nothing whatsoever to do with being part of a family where there is a donor conceived child. It is easy to jump to the conclusion that it may be the underlying reason for things like emotional or behaviour problems, developmental delays or difficulties at school. It is possible that the way your family was created (you or your child's response or attitude to it) may be a contributory factor, but the experience of Network families is that most times there are other explanations. All families go through periods of discomfort, pain or difficulty as well as shared joy and happiness. It is part of normal human development and growth. Families created both with and without donor help are no different.

And finally... As a parent it is easy to feel bad about not being able to provide everything your child wants...including full answers to questions about origins or difference. Don't be too hard on yourself. By being honest, listening, acknowledging feelings and generally being there for them, you are doing everything you can to provide them with the tools (resilience, high self-esteem, self-awareness) to cope with whatever life throws at them.

Glossary

AID

Artificial Insemination by Donor. This was the term used to describe sperm donation before the Human Fertilisation and Embryology Act of 1990.

Biological parent

This is not strictly a scientific term. 'Biologically related' would be more accurate but it could be used to refer to any adult who has provided eggs or sperm to create a child. Where donor eggs are used, the woman who has carried and given birth to a child is sometimes referred to in this way. 'Biological parent' is often used by donor conceived people to refer to 'my biological mum or dad', ie. their donor. In the latter case it tends to be shortened to 'bio mum or dad'. It is also sometimes used to refer to a host surrogate mother whose eggs have not been used to conceive the child.

Co-parent or Co-parenting

A parenting arrangement where two or more people who are not in a formal relationship and may or may not share a sexuality, commit to parent a child probably conceived via donation.

DI Donor Insemination

A term commonly used for sperm donation following the HFE Act 1990. It is used less often these days.

DCA

Donor conceived adult

Donor

Someone who voluntarily gives a part of themselves (such as sperm, eggs, an embryo, blood, an organ) for use by another person

Different types of Donor

Altruistic donor

Those men and women who give their sperm or eggs without needing treatment themselves. In the UK they may receive expenses but not payment for their gametes.

Anonymous donor

Donor to whom a donor conceived child or their parents has no right to identifying information. Some non-identifying information may be available. Since April 2005 UK donors cannot be anonymous. They are paid expenses. Most donors abroad are anonymous.

Egg share donor

Egg share donors are women under 35 who are having IVF treatment themselves, often for male fertility issues, and who agree to share their eggs with one or two women who are in need of donated eggs. This is usually in return for a reduced fee on their own cycle of treatment but many women are also happy to help other women going through similar difficulties.

Identifiable donor

Donor who is anonymous to the recipient at the time of donation but is willing to be known to the child from age 18. All donors at UK licensed clinics have had to be identifiable since 2005.

ID release donor

Donor whose identity will be made available at a specified time to the recipient and/or offspring. See above for UK rules on when the identity of the donor may be made available. These rules may differ in other countries

Known donor

Donor whose identity is known at the time of donation. They can be a friend or family member and may donate at a licensed clinic or, if a sperm donor, privately outside the licensed clinic system.

Private donor

These are sperm donors who donate outside of the regulated system (either anonymously or identifiably). They may be recruited via introduction web sites or through friendship networks.

Diblings	Affectionate term developed in the States to refer to half-siblings by donor conception being raised in other families or half-sibs in the family of the donor.
Donor conceived	Created via the donation of sperm, egg or embryo.
Donor conception	The act of creating a baby using donated sperm, eggs or embryos.
Donor offspring	Babies, children and adults who have been conceived with the help of donated eggs, sperm or embryos.
Double donation	Where eggs and sperm from donors chosen by the recipient are used to create an embryo which is then transferred to a woman's uterus.
DNA	Material that carries all the information about how a living thing will look and function. It is found in every cell of the human body. DNA is short for deoxyribonucleic acid.
DNA testing	Increasingly available via kits sent to your home, these tests can help with a search for genetic relatives and/or be used for health information.
Egg donor	A woman who donates eggs in order to help another woman conceive a child.
Embryo	A collection of cells developed from a fertilised egg, in the early phase of development towards becoming a foetus.
Embryo donation	There are two types of embryo donation. The first, sometimes available in the UK, is where embryos that are not going to be used by a creating couple or individual are frozen and then donated to another person or couple. Donated eggs or sperm may or may not have been used in the creation of the embryos. The second, common in clinics abroad, is where an embryo or embryos are created by a clinic with eggs and sperm from separate donors and then transferred to the uterus of a recipient woman.
Fertilisation	The union (coming together) of a human egg and sperm to produce a zygote – a fertilised egg.
Foetus	The unborn young of a human from the end of the eighth week after fertilisation to the moment of birth.
Gametes	Term used to refer to both eggs and sperm. Although embryos are not strictly gametes they are often included.
Gene	A particular section or portion of a cell's DNA. Genes are coded instructions for making everything the body needs, especially proteins.
Genetic connection	Term used to refer to people who share some DNA, often, though not inevitably, through using the same donor or having a 'blood' relative in common.
Genetic parent	Scientifically accurate term used to refer to a person whose eggs or sperm are used to create a child. It is often used in relation to one of the partners in a parenting couple, a solo mother who has used sperm donation or by a donor conceived person in relation to their donor. It could also refer to a surrogate mother in a 'traditional' surrogacy where the surrogates' eggs have been used for conception
Half-sibling(s)	People that have been conceived with the help of the same donor but raised in different families or children in the family of the donor.

IVF	IVF stands for In vitro fertilisation. It is the process used to create an embryo (potential foetus) outside the body. A woman's eggs and man's sperm are placed together in a plastic dish for fertilisation. The fertilised egg or eggs (now embryos) are then placed in a woman's uterus.
ICSI	Intra-cytoplasmic Sperm Injection: A procedure used to extract a single sperm from the ejaculate or testes of a man in order to inject it into a woman's egg with the intent to create an embryo. It is largely used in cases of severe male fertility problems and requires the IVF process as well.
Selective reduction	A procedure to reduce the number of foetuses being carried by a woman in order to give the remaining ones the best chance of survival. It happens most often following the replacement of more than two embryos in IVF treatment. Clinics in the UK and the EU rarely transfer more than two embryos. See One at a Time www.oneatatime.org.uk
SMC	A solo mother by choice. A single woman who chooses to become a mother without a partner.
Sperm donor	A man who donates his sperm in order to help a person or couple conceive a baby.
Surrogacy	When a woman carries and gives birth to a baby for a couple or individual (referred to as intending parents) who are for a range of reasons, unable to carry a child themselves.

Surrogacy – different types

Host or gestational surrogacy	This is when IVF is used, either with the eggs of the intended mother or with donor eggs. The surrogate mother therefore does not use her own eggs and is genetically unrelated to the baby. Sperm is provided by the intending father.
Straight or traditional surrogacy	This is the simplest and least expensive form of surrogacy. The surrogate mother uses an insemination kit to become pregnant using the intended father's sperm. The baby will be conceived using the surrogate mother's egg and she will, therefore, be genetically related to the baby.
Tandem cycle	A fertility procedure involving embryos being created using a woman's own eggs and eggs from a donor at the same time. If there are viable embryos from both sources then a mixture may be transferred to a woman's uterus. This can result in the recipient not being sure if any resulting pregnancy and child has been created with her own eggs or those from a donor. This treatment is banned in the UK and the EU for ethical reasons.
Twins – fraternal	Two babies born from the same pregnancy who developed from two separate eggs fertilised by two separate sperm cells. They will have non-identical genetic codes.
Twins – identical	Two babies born from the same pregnancy who developed from a single fertilised egg that split, creating two embryos. They share an almost identical genetic code. Always the same gender.
Vasectomy	A surgical procedure for men used as a method of birth control – meaning they can no longer be a genetic parent. The process can sometimes be reversed via a surgical procedure.

Further Reading

Some books, by their publication date, may appear to be rather old. They are included here because I am unaware of anything more contemporary that surpasses the knowledge and wisdom to be found within their covers. Most of the social and emotional issues around donor conception have remained the same for many years, despite the fertility world having changed significantly in so many other ways.

- Kate Brian.
  Precious Babies: Pregnancy, Birth and Parenting after Infertility
  (Piatkus 2011)

- Ken Daniels. *Building a family with the assistance of donor insemination*
  (Dunmore Press, Palmerston North, 2004)

- Diane Ehrensaft. *Mommies, daddies, donors, surrogates: answering tough questions and building strong families*
  (The Guilford Press, New York London, 2005)

- Ellen Sarasohn Glazer
  The long-awaited stork: a guide to parenting after infertility
  (Jossey-Bass Publishers, San Francisco, 1998)

- Ellen Sarasohn Glazer and Evelina Weidman Sterling. *Having your baby through egg donation*
  (Second edition, Jessica Kingsley Publishers, London, 2013)

- Wendy Kramer and Naomi Cahn, J.D.
  Finding our famiies: A first-of-its-kind book for donor conceived people and their families
  (Penguin group, New York, 2013)

- Caroline Lorbach. *Experiences of Donor Conception: Parents, offspring and donors through the Years*
  (Jessica Kingsley Publishers, 2002)

- Olivia Montuschi.
  'You're not my father anyway...'
  March 2005, in Personal Stories on the Donor Conception Network website: www.dcnetwork.org

- Mikki Morrissette. *Choosing single motherhood the thinking woman's guide*
  (Be-Mondo Publishing, Minneapolis, 2005)

For those who like ideas and research studies

All the following are insightful and very accessible.

- Petra Nordqvist and Carol Smart.
  Relative Strangers: Family life, genes and donor conception
  (Palgrave MacMillan Hampshire, 2014)

- Katherine Fine (editor). *Donor Conception for Life: Psychoanalytic Reflections on New Ways of Conceiving the Family*
  (Karnac London, 2015)

- Susan Golombok. *Modern Families: Parents and Children in New Family Forms*
  (Cambridge University Press, Cambridge, 2015)

- Michael E Lamb, University of Cambridge.
  Mothers, Fathers, Families and Circumstances: Factors Affecting Children's Adjustment: Applied Developmental Science 16.2, 98-111, 2012

  This article is a meta-analysis of very many studies about the many factors that affect children's adjustment. It includes and refers specifically to children in new family forms.
  Available to DCN members from the library of DC Network.

Parenting and child development

- Andrea Clifford-Poston. *The secrets of successful parenting: understand what your child's behaviour is really telling you*
  (How to Books, Oxford, 2002)

- Adele Faber and Elaine Mazlish. *How to talk so kids will listen and listen so kids will talk*
  (Piccadilly Press, 2001)
  One of the best parenting books once your child is out of infancy.

- Sue Gerhardt. *Why love matters: how affection shapes a baby's brain*
  (Brunner-Routledge, Hove and New York, 2004)

- Graham Music.
  Nurturing Natures: Attachment and Children's Emotional, Sociocultural and Brain Development
  (Psychology Press 2011)

- Daniel J. Siegel and Mary Hartzel.
  Parenting from the Inside Out: How a deeper self-understanding can help you raise children who thrive
  (Tarcher/Penguin 2004)

Books to help explain about sex and reproduction

For parents

- Dr. Miriam Stoppard. *Questions children ask: and how to answer them*
  (Dorling Kindersley, London, 1997)

For parents and children

- Babette Cole. *Mummy laid an egg*
  (Red Fox, London, 1993)

- Babette Cole. *Mummy never told me*
  (Red Fox, London, 2003)

Books to help explain about donor conception – for parents and children

Our Story

The Donor Conception Network has published a series of story books for young children about their origins in simple, positive language.

- *Children conceived by sperm, egg or double/embryo donation in heterosexual families* (3 books)
- *Children conceived by sperm donation in solo mum families*
- *Children conceived by sperm donation in lesbian parent families*
- *Children conceived by double/embryo donation in solo mum families* (customisable for twins etc...)
- *Children conceived by double/embryo donation in lesbian parent families* (customisable for twins etc...)

Telling and Talking with Children 0-7 yrs
This book provides parents with a source of practical guidance and emotional support in finding the right time and the right language to 'tell' and continue conversations with their children over the years.

Telling and Talking with Friends and Family,
One guide for parents helping them to explain to the wider community about how they conceived their children and one guide *(Our Family)* to give to relatives and friends to help them understand.
(Donor Conception Network, 2013)

All these books are available from the online SHOP at dcnetwork.org

Other books

- Janice Grimes. *X, Y, and me*
  series of story books for children born into many different family and donation types
  (available from www.xyandme.com)

- Tim Appleton.
  My Beginnings: A very special story
  (IFC Resources Centre: available from www.mybeginnings.org)

  This resource, which is available with a CD rom, can be adapted for many different assisted reproduction situations. It is aimed at the older child who may be more interested in the scientific and technical aspects of assisted reproduction and is especially valuable for children conceived via embryo donation, for whom there are few resources available.

- Patricia Sarles, a US based librarian, has put together a long list of books for donor conceived children and their families at
  booksfordonoroffspring.blogspot.co.uk

Further Reading

Books about different sorts of families

- Todd Parr,
  The Family Book and *It's Okay to be Different*
  (Little, Brown Young Readers, 2010 and Little, Brown Young Readers, 2009)

- Cory Silverberg, *What makes a baby: a book for every kind of family and every kind of kid*
  (Zoball Press, 2015)
  Also available is an excellent *Reader's Guide* also by Cory Silverberg which we highly recommend.

- Mary Hoffman with Ros Asquith illustrator.
  Welcome to the Family; different ways a baby or child can come into a family
  (Frances Lincoln Publishers, 2014)

Films

A Different Story...Revisited DVD
(Donor Conception Network 2014)

Contains two films, one featuring children and young people from heterosexual couple families and the other from solo mum and lesbian families. All talk about their thoughts and feelings on being donor conceived.

Telling and Talking about Donor Conception DVD
(Donor Conception Network 2006)

Parents and children talk about their experiences of telling. Includes couples (heterosexual and lesbian) and solo mums.

Both films are available to buy from the online SHOP at dcnetwork.org

Archie Nolan: Family Detective

A funny illustrated story for 8-12yr olds

Science geek Archie Nolan tries to keep a low profile, but when his class are told to research their family tree, he is terrified twin sister and school swot Jemima is going to reveal that they are donor conceived. Archie's in turmoil. He doesn't want to talk about all that embarrassing stuff. The only person who understands is his donor conceived friend Cameron, but he seems to have unearthed a village vampire…. and Archie's far more interested in investigating that!

Open Archie's secret diary and join him and his friends on an action-packed adventure to find out what family really means.

This is a great resource for donor conception families, exploring themes of difference, friendship, connection and family. It's meant to be a conversation starter and is a great companion to this Telling and Talking booklet.

Available from our online shop
Please look on our website for more details about the book, who it's aimed at and what topics it covers.

The Donor Conception Network

The Donor Conception Network provides support and resources to anyone who is thinking about using or who has used egg, sperm or embryo donation to have children. We work directly with families and donor conceived people but also advocate on their behalf, advising clinics, policy makers and other professional bodies.

We are primarily a membership organisation offering contact, community, support and information to donor conception families around the world. Our members range from people at the very early stages of thinking about donor conception to those with adult children now having families of their own.

Our website also provides a wealth of information and guidance. We have an online shop selling books and films for donor conception families including books for young children – the *Our Story* range – and our new book for 8–12yr olds *"Archie Nolan: Family Detective"*.

We publish our Journal twice a year, have a monthly newsletter, run two family conferences in the UK for members each year as well as organising a range of local groups all around the UK. We also offer online contact to members who don't live in the UK or near a local group. We run workshops for those considering donor conception as well as Telling and Talking Workshops for those who have children. Our range of books will continue to expand as our resources allow.

Most importantly we work hard to ensure that donor conception families are represented, their voices are heard, and that donor conception is openly understood by the wider community as one of many ways a family can be created or expanded.

Donor Conception Network

Join us to be part of an organisation proudly supporting and championing you and families like yours.

For information about membership or to make a donation towards our work please visit our website.

Useful Contacts

British Infertility Counselling Association (BICA)
Website, including *Find a Counsellor* facility: www.bica.net
info@bica.net

Donor Sibling Registry
www.donorsiblingregistry.com

A not-for-profit registry and internet forum group started in 2000 by
Wendy Kramer and her DI conceived son Ryan in the US.

The aim is for donor conceived people or their parents (for those
under 18) to make connections with half-siblings, or their donor, by
mutual consent. Open to those who have conceived in the UK and
elsewhere in the world, although main links made are through donor
numbers, not currently available in the UK.

Family Futures
Family Futures Consortium Ltd
3 & 4 Floral Place
7-9 Northampton Grove
Islington
London
N1 2PL

020 7354 4161
Fax: 020 7704 6200
contact@familyfutures.co.uk
www.familyfutures.co.uk

Family Futures is an adoption and adoption support agency providing
therapeutic support for children and parents. They also have an
understanding of the needs of donor conception families.

Human Fertilisation and Embryology Authority (HFEA)
10 Spring Gardens
London
SW1A 2BU

020 7291 8200
Fax: 020 7291 8201
admin@hfea.gov.uk
www.hfea.gov.uk